CHLOE MYERS

Work Hard, Play Hard, Rest Hard

To Oscar and Charlie,
my favourite playmates.
Don't grow up, it's a trick.
Mum x

The one thing that you have that no-body else has is you. Your voice, your mind, your story, your vision. So write and draw and build and play and dance and live as only you can.

Neil Gaiman

Foreword

Integrating the concept of play into our fast-paced and demanding lives may seem unattainable. In a world filled with overwhelming challenges and distractions, the idea of prioritizing play often takes a backseat.

However, after working for 20 years with young people and their parents in war-zones, classrooms, the community and the workplace, as a teacher, coach and play therapist, I know play has the power to transform our lives for good.

Chloe's infectious exuberance and genuine openness is both heartwarming and inviting. She embodies the very essence of someone who has granted herself permission to place play at the forefront and seamlessly infuse it into every aspect of her life.

Our paths intertwined when my mother-in-law shared my work with Chloe. Intrigued, she embarked on the professionals PAUSE, PLAY, CONNECT ® course and soon after, our connection deepened. Chloe then became my coach for a season, guiding me through a transformative journey as I ventured back into the classroom as a secondary music teacher. Within a few sessions, I underwent a remarkable shift in my mindset: from "I have to teach" to "I get to teach." Armed with the principles of my PAUSE, PLAY, CONNECT ® model, I returned to the classroom with renewed enthusiasm, and used this season to incorporate more play-based learning into lessons, improving

i

engagement and behaviour among my students and colleagues alike.

Today, as Play-focused coaches, Chloe and I are truly grateful for our growing partnership. We find ourselves working in extraordinary times, where individuals are time-poor, financially constrained, and experiencing a sense of disconnection from themselves and others. Yet, in the midst of these challenges, we have witnessed the extraordinary power of pausing to play and its ability to rebuild connection, balance and spark joy effectively.

Within the pages of this book, you will discover a transformative blend of ingredients that can propel you forward into a life of ease and flow. However, it will require both discipline and vulnerability to pause and truly engage with the thought-provoking questions that Chloe has thoughtfully positioned throughout your reading journey.

Prepare to embark on a captivating exploration, guided by Chloe's expertise and infectious passion for play. As you delve into the rich content ahead, may you find inspiration, practical insights, joyous storytelling and a renewed appreciation for the role of play in our lives. Remember, it is through embracing the power of play that we can unlock our true potential, foster meaningful connections, and ultimately create a life worth savouring.

Have a play-fuelled day - with permission to play your way,

Debi John

Play Pollinator and Founder of Play Healing CIC

Introduction

Life is busier than ever. It can be hard trying to balance every-thing properly and still find time for fun, play and creativity.

Rest can be equally elusive. There are so many other things to do that can often feel more important: work (whether you love it or hate it), family, keeping the house clean and tidy, eating right, exercising, socialising, hobbies...

It's exhausting.

But what happens when you deprioritise play and rest?

You get overwhelmed and burned out.

You feel like you can't do anything right. You're not doing your best at work. Then, when you get home, you're too tired to do much more than slump down on the sofa with a big bowl of pasta or mindlessly shovel crisps and wine down your neck, while scrolling through social media to distract you from worrying about all the things you should be doing instead. Then you feel guilty for wasting yet another evening. You're so busy worrying about what you didn't get done today and what you have to do tomorrow that you can't sleep properly. You've been staring at bright screens and under artificial light for most of the day and evening, so your brain doesn't know it's time to switch off.

Even your hobbies can feel like a chore – you craft or learn new skills so that one day you could start a dream business and finally escape the job you hate. You exercise to keep fit or because you need headspace or because it's the only time you see your friends – not because you enjoy it.

It doesn't have to be this way.

When you play, you properly relax into the moment, not worrying about the past or future. You enter a mindful and restful flow state. You decompress from today and prepare for tomorrow. You better connect with yourself, with nature, and with your loved ones. Your mind finds the space to wander and see things from different perspectives, so you can come up with more creative and innovative solutions to your problems.

But before you can play, you need to first switch off from work, and take some time to pause, rest and reflect. It's very hard to play when you're feeling stressed or anxious, so learning to set better work boundaries, and to actively rest needs to happen first.

Play looks different for everyone. I define it as something you do purely for the fun of it, for no other purpose than pleasure. Something you can lose yourself in, forgetting all of your worries and losing track of time. Not with a view to getting fit or making money, but simply because it brings a smile to your face.

For you, play might be dancing, piano or chess, painting, skinny dipping in the sea, having a tickle fight with your kids, having a kickabout in the park, building a sandcastle, a walk in the woods, hula hooping, banter at work, flirting, sex... It doesn't have to be high energy or what you traditionally think of as fun either: it might be meditation or yoga, cooking or gardening, even cleaning – if you're that way inclined.

Play can be free and simple, and it might only last for a moment.

As soon as you create more time for play, your life feels lighter, your problems smaller, your goals more achievable. Some of those goals no longer even matter because you enjoy your life more as it is; you have less desire or need for change. Your purpose and your priorities become clearer.

Sounds simple enough.

Just play more. Easy peasy.

But it's often easier said than done. You've been trained to be productive and busy all the time. Otherwise, you are being lazy, right?

It's unsustainable. You can't keep it up forever. Burnout and overwhelm become inevitable.

To find the space for play, to give yourself permission to stop doing and just *be*, you first need to work on setting clearer boundaries in every area of your life. You need to look at how you organise your diary and what you are choosing to prioritise, and what you want to change or stop doing altogether. You need to look at the thoughts and worries that are filling your head and causing all this stress. You need to learn to fully switch off from work when you're not working, so that you can engage with whatever it is that you *are* doing. And you need to rest and recharge effectively. This will open up the space and possibility for more play, fun and creativity.

Throughout my career, I've worked with people to discover their passions, reach their goals, and find a better balance. I've worked with people with disabilities who wanted to come off benefits and into employment, and with people who were starting their own small businesses after the world of work just didn't work for them. I've worked with volunteers who wanted to find more meaning and fulfilment in their lives through helping others. I've worked with lonely and vulnerable elderly people with declining health or caring for someone who was sick. I've worked with mums who were trying and failing to fit it all in, with their own self-care usually being the first thing to go. I've led a team of health coaches who supported lonely and isolated people with their health and wellbeing.

I've worked with all of these people to look at their lives holistically, to understand what's really important to them and to make sure they're getting it. I've empowered them to find their own solutions to their problems and to lead happier lives as a result.

All of my experience has made it clear to me that play is essential and under-prioritised. It's shown me that connection is the solution to a whole load of problems. And on my own personal journey, I've discovered the importance of resting and being in the moment.

In this book, I hope to bring together everything I've learned from my career, life, and training, to help you live a happier, healthier life.

Who am I to advise you on how to live your life? I've asked myself this question many times throughout the writing process. I'm not perfect. No-one is. Perfect doesn't exist. There's no one right way to live. But I'm doing my best to find the right way for me, and to help others find their own right way. Writing this is as much to remind myself how I want to live as it is for you or anyone else to learn from.

I want to help you work less and play more. I'm realistic though. I know that quitting work or reducing your hours isn't achievable for most people (in fact, it's more likely you work part time and would like more hours - or at least more income). I believe that more play and more rest will make you more productive in less time at work.

I'm not going to tell you I can teach you how to manifest thousands of pounds with no work on your part, nor am I going to tell you that I can help you earn the same amount you do now in significantly less hours. With the right innovative idea, maybe you can. That's not what this book is about, but if you free up enough space in your life to play, that bright idea might just come to you when you're least expecting it.

My approach is more about accepting and appreciating life as it is, whilst still wanting to grow and develop and taking action to do so. It's about learning to live with less rather than earning and having more. And it's about being grateful for and wanting what you already have, instead of focusing on what you don't have or what you want that is out of reach. It's about setting better boundaries so that your work doesn't seep over into the rest of your life. Those boundaries are what will help you enjoy your downtime, better engage with your kids, sleep better, and generally enjoy life more. Even if you love your job, downtime is what gives your brain a rest so that you can come back to work with fresh perspectives, more creative ideas and innovative solutions.

I want to help you work hard, rest hard, and play hard. I want doing those things hard to become easy. I want to help you be more selfish and live the life you really want, without feeling guilty about it, by recognising that putting yourself first enables you to better look after others.

This book is part of my attempt to achieve a happier, healthier world for us all. It's full of reflection questions to get you thinking. I encourage you to scribble all over your copy and make it a useful resource as you create your more playful, fun, creative, pleasure- and joy- filled future. No need to read it in order either – dip in and out as you wish!

How to Use This Book

This book is in sections. Please use it in the way that suits you best, scribbling your ideas and answers throughout and reading it in any order you like.

Part One is a reflection questionnaire that you can use to reflect on your life as it is now, and start thinking about how you'd like it to be different. You might want to think about the answers, write about them, or talk about them.

Then, in Part Two: The Problem, I share my own story of hitting and escaping burnout.

In Part Three we explore The Solution with a chapter each about work, rest, and play, including some of my own tips and tricks for improving each area so that you can find a better balance between the three.

Then in Part Four we start to think about The Result of finding a better balance. It's also about how you might first need to come to terms with change so that you are ready to take advantage of your new-found free time to set yourself goals that will stretch you outside of your comfort zone towards a happier, more authentic and fulfilling life.

Part Five will introduce you to my own coaching tool, The Hopscotch Method, which will help you visualise your goals and work through the steps you need to make your dreams come true - including your values, beliefs, confidence, and identity.

What do you hope to get from reading this book?

I

Reflection Questionnaire

On the following pages are a series of reflection questions to get you thinking about how you want to design your future. I recommend writing your answers in here now, and returning to them with new answers in the future, say six months from now. You might be surprised how much can change once you start implementing some of the ideas in this book. You might also want to use these as prompts for longer journal posts or conversations with friends.

How do you feel about taking time to reflect?

How would you describe yourself?

How would other people describe you?

How do you want to be remembered at your funeral?

What are you really proud of, personally and/or professionally?

What do you do when life is challenging, and you feel out of control?

What do you do just for the fun and joy
of it?

What would your younger self think of
your life today?

What are you grateful for?

What does your life look like now?

What would you like your life to look like in six months time?

What would you like your life to look like in two years time?

What would you like your life to look like in ten years time?

What assumptions, fears or beliefs are holding you back?

What habits do you want to stop, start, or change?

What will you need to keep from your past to achieve your dream future, and what will you need to leave behind?

What would you do if there was nothing stopping you: if you weren't worried about what others would think, if money were no object, you had time, and knew you couldn't fail?

What's really getting in the way of the
life you have and the life you want?

If your life were portrayed in a film, would you be the main character? What genre of film would it be? What would be the message or moral of the film?

A letter from the future

One of the previous questions was, "What would your younger self think of you?"

Now I want you to imagine your future self, looking back on your life with pride and happiness, having achieved all the things you are thinking about doing right now.

Write yourself a letter from your future self, giving your current self advice, and congratulating them on all they have achieved and learned.

WORK HARD, PLAY HARD, REST HARD

Mirror Mirror

How did it feel to write that letter, to imagine being the you that has achieved everything that you want to, and reflects back on life with pride rather than regret? What do you need to commit to right now, to make this possible?

What are you going to do next, to get one step closer to your dreams?

II

The Problem

It can feel like we are all one major (or not-so-major) event away from burnout. Whilst we're feeling that way, it's hard to take a step back to see the bigger picture and find collective solutions to it. In this section, I share my own burnout story and how I overcame it and improved my life.

What's the main thing causing you stress right now? And what's the main thing bringing you joy?

My Story

Burnout hit me in Autumn 2021.

On the surface I was still functioning. I was getting my work done, my kids were clean and fed, and I was smiling. When I was in public, at least. At home, I was most likely found lying in bed, exhausted and unmotivated.

One day, I was on my way to go rowing with friends. As I walked, I started crying – the tears appearing on my cheeks before I even realised what was happening. I remember feeling determined to just let myself cry and get it all out before I arrived to meet the others.

I pulled myself together as I arrived at the boat, only for my friend Carol to ask how I was. The tears instantly started rolling again. Carol gave me a massive healing hug and I let it all out.

I don't tend to show my emotions like that in public often. I'm generally positive and optimistic even in the hardest times. So, when I do, people understand that things are bad. I got my tears out, and climbed into the boat and lost myself in the pull of the oars against the wind and tide. It was just what I needed to clear my head.

I knew something needed to change, but I didn't know what. It felt impossible.

I was working at a local charity and it was busier than ever. I was the leader. They needed me strong and healthy, setting an example of good wellbeing. We were still in the pandemic. My dad was sick, so I was trying to visit him three times a week to help walk the dog, do some shopping, and get him to his various medical appointments. My mum had died in July 2020, the day we came out of the first lockdown, and what would have been her 62nd birthday was coming up.

My eldest son, Oscar, was school-refusing. Every morning was a struggle and a fight to get him to school, often only to end up with him home with me for the day whilst I tried to work. Other times he'd convince us to drive him to school (only a ten minute walk, even at his slow pace!) only to be physically unable to get out of the car, or to do it and immediately panic and jump back in. I didn't really mind having him around, he was easy and pleasant company once school was given up on for the day, but I wasn't able to focus on him or my work properly so I was constantly frustrated at both.

My youngest son, Charlie, was just getting on with it, getting himself dressed and off to school each morning completely independently. I was worried about Oscar and felt constantly guilty about not giving Charlie more of my time and attention.

My wonderful husband, Steve, was holding everything to-gether: doing all the cleaning, cooking, making packed lunches, food shopping, sorting out play dates and birthday presents.

I felt absolutely helpless and useless. I wasn't able to do anything as well as I wanted to. I felt like was failing in every area of my life.

Watching my baby having such a difficult time took up all of my attention. I wasn't able to focus on anything else properly.

In an attempt to improve things, I attended a Trauma Release Exercise (TRE) class after hearing about it from a friend. It's a technique often used with military veterans who have a lot of trauma but don't feel able to talk about it and likely wouldn't seek talk therapies. Other mammals shake after experiencing a traumatic event, and, as mammals, our bodies want to do this too. But we have been conditioned not to shake, so we hold it in instead. Through TRE we allow our bodies to follow this impulse and release stress that has sometimes been trapped and pushed down inside us for years. Think of other times that you might shake: when you're cold, a big ugly cry, uncontrollable laughter, a perfect orgasm. You feel better, happier, and more relaxed after a shake of any kind.

As well as teaching me how to practice TRE at home, the teacher, Jo, helped me understand the awful cycle Oscar and I were in. He was anxious about school. I was worried about him. He'd see that I was worried and then he'd feel guilty and even more worried. Then I'd get more worried when I saw how anxious he was...

I needed to look after myself, to show him that I was calm and relaxed and that it was safe for him to relax too. At work, I constantly told my team, "You can't pour from an empty cup." I was too wrapped up in my life to see the wood for the trees and understand that was exactly what I'd been trying to do. I needed some distance to get a new perspective.

Eventually I went to the doctor and was signed off work for a couple of weeks. I hadn't wanted to take time off. Work had felt like the only place I was succeeding or had any control. But it was also the only thing that I felt could change. In that couple of weeks, I wholeheartedly threw myself into medically prescribed self-care (I have fairly simple needs: a spa day and a haircut and some big walks by the sea).

I went back to work, but only for a week or two before I realised it wasn't sustainable. I knew something had to change, but I still couldn't see what or how.

In my return to work meeting, over many cups of tea, my Chair of Trustees, Alwyn, asked what the biggest cause of stress was for me. It was undoubtedly Oscar's wellbeing and education.

She told me that she'd home educated her grandson and showed me for the first time that this was a real option. School had felt like a necessity, just what people do. With the fear of parental fines if you dared take your child out of school in term-time or have them off sick too often, it felt like a legal obligation to send my children to school. I'd never questioned it.

When I stopped to properly think about it, suddenly it became clear that I didn't really know why Oscar was going to school. He was barely in lessons when he was there, and when he did brave the classroom, he was too anxious and dysregulated to actually learn anything. Lessons were mainly spent working quietly alone, and he spent lunchtimes away from his friends, so he wasn't at school to socialise. In earlier years, school was at least partly about childcare, but I had him with me most of the time now anyway, and he was old enough to be alone if necessary.

Following that meeting, over the space of about seventy-two hours, I turned my entire life upside down: I took Oscar out of school for good, quit my job, and signed up to do an accredited coaching course. I'd been looking into becoming a coach for some time. Coaching my team was hands down my favourite part of my work. I loved challenging them to reach their potential and helping them problem solve. And I had a chip on my shoulder about never having been to university, so being able to get myself a Masters Level qualification was a dream come true for me. I kept telling myself, "If I'd signed up for this two years ago, I'd already be qualified by now." It was important to me to have something of my own and to have an identity beyond being a mum.

It was risky and scary and I'm so grateful to have had Steve's love and support throughout, even though it put a lot more financial pressure on him. It is absolutely possible to home educate and still work (perhaps your income pays for tutors and classes, or your child is able to learn independently, or you juggle work and home educating with your partner). That was my original intention, but it became clear that I needed a major change just as much as Oscar did, so leaving work was right for me.

My upbringing (more about that later) taught me that money isn't necessary for happiness and that it's okay to take your own path in life, to seek out love and adventure rather than money and status. Understanding my values and what was important to me (something coaching gave me) helped me make my decisions quickly, confident that they were the right ones.

I haven't looked back for a second: Oscar is back to being a happy lovely boy and has grown in confidence; our whole household is calmer; and I'm better connected with Charlie, whom I'm now much closer to. A real unintended positive consequence to choosing to home educate Oscar!

We have a little less money but so much more time for each other; and I have loved every single second of my coaching journey. Oscar has often been a willing sounding board for my business ideas and a guinea pig for me to practice new coaching tools on. I can see the impact of it on him too as he will ask me open, curious questions and leave plenty of patient silence as I process my answers. He is a little coach in the making! Throughout my course and beyond, I have also been a guinea pig for many trainee coaches, giving me insight into different styles of coaching and keeping my own balance in check too!

I'm grateful to my burnout.

Burnout forced me to reassess everything in my life and shake things up to make them better. If it hadn't got as bad as it did, I might have carried on struggling away indefinitely. I hope that you might be able to shake your life up without having to reach your breaking point first.

My story isn't unusual. The specifics might be unique to me, but the general feeling of overwhelm and burnout is one that is becoming more and more common, even expected, and inevitable.

People are working full time in jobs they've studied hard for and put their hearts and souls into for years, and they are still having to use food banks. (Teachers, nurses: I'm looking at you.) As I write this in December 2022, we are in the midst of a cost of living crisis following Brexit and the pandemic. Desperate people who are relying on desperate food banks are having to ask not to be given soup because they can't afford to heat it up.

It isn't right that anyone should be in that kind of poverty, and especially not people who are working full time. How did it come to this?

When you're having to fight for your basic survival needs, there's understandably no energy left for "being your best self" or "living your best life." There's nothing left to drive you to make changes to your own life or campaign for more from your government. Every day is a struggle for survival.

And yet, I grew up in these kinds of conditions. We had no central heating: I lived permanently in my sleeping bag to keep warm. Our TV only had four channels and no remote, even whilst all our friends seemed to be getting big Sky dishes put up on their houses. My dad wasn't around; he was usually out of the country, and he didn't provide financially so there was a huge pressure on Mum, who was working three or four jobs at a time.

I loved my childhood though. I don't have any unhappy memories. We didn't have nice things, and that meant we were free to be messy. We could paint and get muddy and build dens with a sheet over the clothes horse and the back of the sofa. We were outdoors a lot, having picnics, building sandcastles, splashing in puddles, collecting frog spawn. We got books out of the library instead of ordering them from Amazon. My childhood uniform was a pink felt hat Mum got in a charity shop, and my brother, Jake, spent a good year wearing nothing but the bumble bee outfit Mum made him for his fourth birthday party.

When we did see Dad, he'd take us off caving or abseiling. We'd always have a proper adventure, coming home exhausted and plastered in mud.

Life was pretty idyllic as far as I was concerned. Money would almost certainly have made things easier on my mum, but I'm not sure what the impact would have been on my happiness.

Even right up to the end of Mum's life, she was always mindfully appreciating rainbows or the changing leaves on the trees, and she was forever grateful to friends and the NHS for all they did for her. Gratitude is hardwired in me and it has served me well.

What I'm trying to say is; it doesn't matter how rubbish life seems, there's always room for more gratitude, playfulness and joy to brighten it up. In this book I hope to give you lots of practical ideas, most of them free or low cost, to help you infuse your life with more mindfulness, gratitude, play, creativity, joy, rest, and connection.

III

The Solution

It feels like there are so many suggestions out there to help us with our wellbeing. It can be expensive and overwhelming in itself! In this section, I will provide some simple and low-cost suggestions to help you better work hard, rest hard, and play hard.

What do you do to look after yourself?

Work

First, take some time to reflect on your current work situation.

What do you love about your work? What is your biggest challenge at work? What would you like to change? How much do you think about work when you're not there? What do you want to achieve at work this year?

Work Hard

When I say "work," I mean all the things you *have* to do. The things you need to do, must do, should do.

Don't all those phrases just make you instantly groan, before you've even considered what the endings of them might be?

For you, this chapter might be about work, or at least parts of your job or running your business. It might be about educating your children or caring for your parents. It might be about staying on top of the never-ending household chores: food shopping, cooking, cleaning, laundry, birthday cards, and life admin. It's about the things you'd pay an assistant to do if money were no object.

You might love doing some of things that you have to do, but at the end of the day, you don't have that much choice whether you do them or not. There are consequences to face if they aren't done.

Do you know how and when you work best? Maybe it's the morning, the afternoon, or the evening. Or perhaps you can only work effectively after you've had a workout or fresh air. Do you work better quietly on your own or do you prefer to have others around you to bounce ideas off and to motivate you? Is music a distraction or does it keep you focused? What difference does a lunchbreak make to your day - does it give you a fresh burst of energy, make you sleepy, or make you lose your flow? Do you like to work in short bursts every day or cram it all into as few days as possible so you can have full days off in the week?

Home education allows us to work around Oscar's moods and motivations (and mine). If he's tired in the morning, I'll get some work done and do things with him in the afternoon. If he's feeling driven to work on a project during the evening or weekend, we can go with that. After working hard on something for half an hour, he might be exhausted and need a break. If he's really into something, he might want to carry on with it all day. He wasn't able to work like that in school. He would have shut down instead, present in body but not in mind. Through home education, we have been able to change the environment instead of trying to change him. We make it work for him, and for all of us.

Oscar and I have found our rhythm, rather than a routine. It's more fluid and flexible than trying to stick to the same pattern each day or week. And it ties in better with my cycle too – I get so tired the day before my period. I now have the flexibility to take the rest I need on those days, to be kind to myself and not take on any challenging tasks that will just leave me frustrated and grumpy. When I was drinking and the start of my period coincided with a hangover, these days were frankly awful, but now they are much more manageable and I'm more in tune with my body and what it needs.

I always found working during the school holidays incredibly difficult too. I was lucky in how well I was supported with childcare, so it wasn't a practical issue. I just felt like everyone else was out having lovely holidays and days out with their children in the sun. (Blame social media! Of course I knew it was only the people who were doing fun things who were sharing them, and plenty of others were working just like me, but it didn't always feel like it.) I was always less productive when I worked during school holidays because I felt unmotivated, resentful and guilty all at once.

I loved my job. I was leading a small charity to support lonely and vulnerable people to live happier and healthier lives. It was rewarding and fulfilling. I worked with amazing, kind, hard-working, dedicated, and passionate people. Every day was different and interesting. I had the freedom and flexibility to do school runs and watch school plays and cheer my kids on at sports days and meet friends for lunch. I worked a short walk from home, and at home when I wanted to. The job was challenging and stretchy for me. I was valued by my team, my trustees, and my community. There was nothing that I could or would have changed to make it better. It was about as perfect as a job could get.

But even in a dream job, it was hard to keep good boundaries. People who choose to work or volunteer for a charity are passionate and they really care about their cause. They can find it hard to switch off. When you're meeting people in need all day, you can often go home and worry about them and wish there was more you could do help them. It's often easier to notice all the ways in which you weren't able to help them than it is to celebrate the ways you have already helped them.

Even in more administrative roles, you're very aware of the importance of your role, and the financial pressures the charity is under. You want to do everything you can to ensure that things keep running smoothly, and that the fundraising keeps coming in and the expenditure is kept to a minimum.

In a paid position in a charity, you're all too aware of the hard work volunteers are doing every day for free, so most charity workers put in far more than their contracted (and often low paid in the first place) hours.

I wanted to lead by example. My team saw me taking proper lunch breaks every day, leaving on time every day, attending personal appointments and school events without feeling guilty or apologetic about it.

It was still all-consuming though. I would spend my non-working hours coming up with ideas or wanting to carry on with a project I was working on. I was available to my staff by phone when they needed me, whenever that might be. They might not have often contacted me on days off, but they could have done and when they did they expected a response. That meant I was always "on call" and in work-mode. I didn't often fully switch off from work.

I loved my job. I loved pretty much every single part of it (especially once someone else took over all the spreadsheets and accounts so that I only needed to review them rather than create them!). The things that I was thinking about when I wasn't working were usually things I was excited about and genuinely wanted to do, not things I was stressed or worried about. But it doesn't matter how much you love your job if there is no boundary between it and the rest of your life. This was hardest during lockdown when everyone was at home (aka at work) all the time, and so many people were suffering with loneliness and anxiety. It felt like there was no excuse for not replying to a phonecall or email promptly.

Then I was introduced to Simon Sinek's Golden Circle on a leadership course. It's all about finding your "why" - your purpose - and leading with that. In marketing, that means you start with your vision, your dream, your mission, and then follow with your products or services and their features.

If you are selling toothpaste, that's the difference between saying, "We sell toothpaste to help keep your mouth healthy," or "We want to improve your mouth health with our amazing toothpaste." The second one sounds more appealing, and opens the door for them to also sell mouthwash, floss, and gum, rather than twenty different types of toothpaste.

In a work context, it's a really useful tool for your elevator pitch – whether you're an entrepreneur or employee. Instead of introducing yourself with a job title that probably doesn't tell anyone outside of your organisation anything about what you do, how could you sum up your role in one simple sentence that shows your passion and gives a feel for what your job is about? How would you introduce yourself to someone in the pub or at a networking event that would inspire them to be genuinely curious to know more? Does your work elevator pitch fit the rest of your life too? When you find a simple sentence that sums up your work, hobbies, and lifestyle, you know you've hit the authenticity jackpot!

I instantly started using The Golden Circle for absolutely everything. Every job description, every meeting, every project, every task, every email. I'd ask myself, "What is the purpose of this? What's the ideal outcome? How will I know if it's been a success?" Try it next time you post on social media. Think about whether you're trying to share some useful information or make people laugh, and how you'll know if it worked. Is it based on the number of likes, comments, or shares? Would just one comment from the right person telling you it genuinely helped them be enough, or do you need ten or one hundred of those?

If what I was doing wasn't directly related to the desired outcome, I was able to question whether it was really necessary at all, and if it was, if there was perhaps someone better suited to take it on. If what I was doing wasn't working, I could think of alternative approaches to it that would still lead to the same desired outcome (I could change the "what" and the "how" whilst still achieving the "why."). If I'd been invited to a meeting, but I couldn't clearly explain what I was going there for – either to offer some knowledge or provide some input, or receive some – then I could seek further clarification or decline it. And I could make sure my team knew why they were going to a meeting too so they could make the same sorts of decisions.

And, particularly during lockdown when life was extra-challenging, I'd set myself one main goal for the day. To catch up with that person so that... To finish that report so that... To make that one phone call so that... As long as I completed that one thing, I'd deem my day a success.

Putting a, "so that," on the end of your sentences is the easiest way to get in touch with why you are doing that thing. If you can't finish the sentence beyond the, "so that," it's time to question whether you should be doing it at all.

Celebrating our small successes is so important. It's all too easy to focus our attention on the things we didn't get done, or that didn't go how we wanted them to, and to forget about the things we did or that went better than planned. What are you really proud of that you've done today? What did you find difficult or frustrating? Which answer came to you more easily?

Discovering the Golden Circle was life-changing for me.

Suddenly I was so much better able to prioritise, plan, and set boundaries for myself. I saved myself hours of attending meetings that weren't relevant to me. I was much clearer on what my job was and what I needed to delegate and who to.

Many people seek coaching because they want to develop their career; they want to go for that big promotion or finally build up the courage to leave the security of the corporate world and follow their entrepreneurial dreams. They want more time with their families, friends, and to spend on their hobbies. Sometimes though, you can get caught in the rat race again, earning more money or building a business, but forgetting what it was all for. Is the money and status worth it if it's costing you time with your children? If you set out in business to make a positive change in the world, is that still at the core of what you do or have you got lost in the race for more money and publicity?

I've worked with people who left their high powered, well paid, corporate jobs to start their own business and have more time with their family, only to find they're spending more time on their business than they did at work. Others have followed the career ladder only to find they hate people management and want to get back to working with customers or patients because that's what brought them into their industry in the first place.

Recently I received some feedback from a client who used to come home after a hard day and spend the evening fretting about work, have a restless sleep because they were worrying about the next day, and then go in tired and more likely to be emotional or make mistakes. After a particularly hard day now with the same triggers as before, she told me that she was able to go food shopping on the way from work, bake brownies with her daughter, and then read her book. She got a decent sleep and woke up ready to face another day.

Being able to read your book and bake a cake might sound like a pretty minor goal, not enough to seek coaching for. But so many of my clients tell me, "I just want to read my book." A big part of that is giving yourself permission to leave the washing up and choose to read instead, but so many of us (especially mums) can find that almost impossible, at least if we don't want to feel guilty about it.

By setting boundaries around her work and giving her a new perspective, this client was able to find time to do the things she wanted to - connecting with her family and relaxing fully. You might have loftier goals than that, but in the end, for most people, the end goal comes down to living a happy and stress-free life shared with loved ones.

To know what you want from work, you first need to get in touch with your career values. What makes work worth it to you? Is it about money, or status, giving something back, developing or using your skills, community? Do you value flexibility so that work fits in with your other responsibilities? Do you need autonomy to be creative in your work, or do you prefer to be given clear tasks and follow instructions? If you were offered two dream job opportunities at the same time, how would you choose one over the other?

Once you know what your career values are, you need to ask yourself if your current role is honouring them. If not, does it have the potential to?

When there is a mismatch between your values and your reality, you feel misaligned, not quite right. If you haven't explored what your career values are, then you won't necessarily understand where that feeling is coming from or what you can do about it.

Once you are in touch with your values and purpose, decision making becomes a whole lot easier. You can identify what's missing from your role, and whether it's possible to get it. Then you can decide to accept things as they are, speak to a manager about changing them, or make the decision to look for alternative work elsewhere which better meets your values and purpose.

If you choose to seek changes in your role or workplace so that your current role can start to meet your values, you might be facing a difficult conversation and not know where to start with it.

This is an exercise I often use in coaching sessions, which you could replicate with a friend or alone in a journal.

Start off by saying all the things you'd say to your employer if you weren't afraid of how they'd react. (This also works for partners, exes, in-laws, difficult customers – any conversation that feels a bit scary!)

Now take away a layer of fear. Imagine that you've just won the lottery, so if you get fired it won't matter.

What would you say this time?

Now for another layer of fear to go.

This time, imagine that not only have you just won the lottery, but you've bumped into your employer after you've had a couple of drinks and have fewer inhibitions.

Time to get all your anger and frustration out!

Now, reflect on what you've said. How do you feel having got your true feelings out? What were the key points? What do you really want to say to that person? Can you sum up your key message, desire, or need in one simple sentence?

That's where to start with your conversation. Get straight to the point. The more you skirt around the problem or act defensively, the more likely the other person will also get defensive and prepared to say no because they expect you to ask for something really difficult.

Once you've asked for what you want, they might surprise you with an instant yes. If they do, brilliant! Then you can get into the details of it.

If you don't get your yes straight away, that's when to start adding some more detail about what you want, why, and how you can see it improving. It's a cliché, but here is where you want to be offering solutions rather than problems. A basic premise of coaching is that the person with the problem is the person with the best solution to that problem – so trust in your own ideas.

Don't give the other person the work of coming up with a solution to a problem they might not even see as a problem. Give them a simple solution that they can say yes or no to.

Because if it's a no, you now know that this job isn't the right cultural fit for you, and it's time to start looking elsewhere.

You can set yourself a boundary: I won't work anywhere that doesn't meet my values. (That doesn't mean quitting your job tomorrow, but it might mean refreshing your CV or LinkedIn profile and starting to look for something else. Unfortunately when you're feeling overwhelmed and burned out and want to find a new job, you're also too exhausted to find the energy to seek out and enthusiastically apply for new jobs.)

Boundary setting is the key to working hard without burning out. If you don't know what your boundaries are, how can you communicate them or recognise when they are being broken?

You need to be clear on what is part of your role and what isn't. When you're asked to do something that isn't within your role, you can decide whether or not to do it. It's not about refusing to do anything outside of your role – some of that is just part of being a team player – but you do need to recognise when you're doing it and think about the impact it might have on your work and wellbeing.

You need to be clear on your boundaries around breaks, lunchtimes, finishing for the day, overtime. Do you see work socials as a fun thing or are they just more work to you? Is there an expectation that you must attend socials outside of work time, or are you putting that on yourself?

Emails too. Pinging emails drag us from what we are really working on, constantly distracting us and making it hard to focus.

When we moved into a new office, we didn't have Internet access for a few weeks. It was heaven! We would check our emails at home in the morning and create a to do list. Then we'd go into work and make our way through all the tasks on that list all day. Then go home and check our emails again. I was so much more productive working that way than in constant firefighting mode, responding to what came in rather than doing what I'd planned to.

Emails just breed more emails.

Checking your emails on a schedule means that you can be more in control of how you are spending your time at work, ensuring that you are being productive and creative.

If necessary, you can use email signatures and auto-responses to set expectations about when people can expect a response, so that they know to call you instead if their email is urgent.

Work Easy

What are your main takeaways from the previous chapter? How could you set better boundaries - even, and perhaps especially, if you love your work?

Rest

Take some time to reflect on the ways that you rest.

How do you like to rest? Which activities energise you and which drain you? Do you sleep well? Do you wake up feeling well rested? Where does your mind go when you stop and do nothing?

Rest Hard

Resting sounds so easy. Increasingly though, it seems that people just don't know how to stop. Life is go, go, go, all the time. There is just so much to get done. You have endless to do lists. Stopping and taking a break is just delaying all the things you "should" be getting on with. It can cause guilt and shame, and leave you feeling lazy. Or you set aside time to take a break but find that your mind is too busy to actually rest and relax. You might even actively choose to keep busy to avoid the thoughts that come into your head when you stop, or to numb them with food, alcohol, or endlessly scrolling through social media.

We all need breaks. Even if you absolutely love your job and are happy pouring your heart and soul into it, you can't keep going forever. Even if you really enjoy cleaning and love having a perfect home, it's not possible to be guest-ready at all times. Even though you love being with your kids, there's no doubt that it's tiring. There's no shame in asking for help – or just admitting that you need it.

Taking a break will leave you rested and ready for the next challenge. It will help you gain new perspectives and ideas. And it will keep you healthy so that you can keep going. Taking a break is a selfless act because it will ultimately benefit your business, children, and whatever other responsibilities you have.

Resting is productive. Self care is selfless. It's only by taking time for yourself that you can continue helping others.

If your to do list looks too overwhelming for a break to feel possible, try splitting it into the following categories to clarify what really needs to be done right now: do, delegate, delay, or ditch. You might be surprised how few things you truly have to do right now.

Now you've got your lists, schedule your tasks into your diary. Leave enough time to allow for procrastination or needing a rest before moving on to the next task. Be kind to yourself and make sure your diary is filled so that it's realistic to achieve everything in it. Schedule tasks like reading or meditating into your diary and honour them as you would any other appointment.

I like to try to organise my days so that I'm working and using my brain in the morning, filling and stretching my brain in the afternoon with learning, and emptying it in the evening by journalling and meditating. That allows me to go to bed clear headed and get a proper sleep so that I'm raring to go the following morning. Sorting out your to do list might be enough to give yourself the permission you need to take a break.

Your break might be as simple as a few slow deep breaths before you speak or make a phone call. It might be leaving your desk to go to the toilet or make a cup of tea. It might be leaving the office for five minutes to get a change of scene and some fresh air. One of my favourites is sitting outside the house when I've got home in the car, listening to the end of a song or podcast and enjoying the gap between work and home, knowing there is no risk of traffic or breakdown, because I'm already so-very-almost home.

A bigger break might be taking a long hot bath, going for a walk in nature, meditating for half an hour, attending a yoga class. Maybe for you, it's taking a nap, having a face mask, booking yourself in for a massage or a haircut. It might be scrolling through social media, watching TV, or chatting with a friend.

I love to go barefoot in nature. There's no greater feeling, especially after a big hike, than taking off your shoes and socks and stretching out your feet. Walking on grass, mud, or sand forces you to slow down and be mindful of your environment, grounding you in the moment.

For many people, writing a journal provides the perfect mindful, head-clearing break. Writing at a regular time of day, like first thing in the morning or last thing at night, can help to make it a habit that you keep up. In his book, Atomic Habits, James Clear suggests Habit Stacking. That is to connect your new habit to an existing habit. For example, "After I brush my teeth, I do five minutes of stretches." Or "Before I check my phone in the morning, I write a page in my journal." Or, my personal favourite, "Before I get in the shower, I clean the toilet."

I only really discovered journalling during lockdown. Each day I'd set myself three goals. I'd review how I'd got on with the previous day's goals. Then I'd summarise how the day had gone: the good, the bad, and the ugly. I'd write what I was stressed about and what I was looking forward to. And I'd list three things I was grateful for. (I've included a template at the end of this book for you to use to give this a try yourself.)

I tried to set myself one goal for myself like exercising or relaxing or catching up with a friend; one for work like attending a meeting or catching up on emails; and one for the family – usually to do with housework or home schooling. Then, if I found myself getting stressed about something, if it wasn't one of my goals for the day, I found it easier to let it go and come back to it another time.

Another journalling technique I have found really useful when I feel overwhelmed is to simply list all the things I am stressed about. Just writing them down eases a little of the stress and gives me headspace. A problem shared is a problem halved, even if you're only sharing it with your journal. I then go back through the list with a different coloured pen and make a note next to each item, such as, "I can't change this, I need to accept it as it is," or, "I can't do anything about this right now," or, "I need to do X to resolve this."

Then I pull out all the, "I need to do," items and I've got a much smaller to do list than I started with and I can use my headings of do, delegate, delay or ditch again if I need to. Next, I go through the list and put the date I plan to do that thing next to each item, and then put the items into my diary on those days for a specific time, which I try to honour just as I would an appointment or meeting. Suddenly life seems a whole lot more manageable!

Nowadays I have less structure and tend to just write to clear my head, letting my mind switch off and my hand take over. I go through phases of journalling a lot or not at all, and it is now one of my favourite ways to find my flow. I know that, in lockdown, the days when I was feeling most stressed and overwhelmed were the days when I hadn't done it. Now, I make an effort to write about the good days and experiences I have as well as the difficult, so that, if I want to, I can look back over my journals in years to come and remember the good times – I'm not sure I'd want to read them if they were all doom and gloom!

After my grandma died, I devoured the letters we found in her house. Beautiful handwritten wartime love letters with tales from her land army days, before and after she met her husband – Grandpops to me.

There is no stack of love letters between my husband and me for anyone to find and read when I die. There are a few postcards from when I was travelling, and a few letters I've written before doing anything adventurous (like the sky dive my friends bought me for my 30th birthday present) just in case I died, but nothing too embarrassing.

My journals are a different matter. In them I can be my worst self. I can be utterly pathetic and whinge and whine to my heart's content. I can be confident and share my wildest dreams and desires without shame. The thought of my children or grandchildren one day reading them is frankly horrifying.

But I can't bring myself to destroy them. What if I want or need to read them back some day? I read them myself, sometimes, if I want to remind myself of harder times and how far I've come.

Journalling feels like a break and a rest to me. It clears my head and relaxes me. A walk or run might do the same for you.

Journalling, walking and other mindful breaks help me connect with myself, who I am and who I want to be. Connecting with ourselves is the first step in overcoming loneliness. Only by knowing your authentic self can you go out and find people on the same wavelength as you and build your tribe.

Once my head is clear, I am in a much better position to truly relax. To actively relax. That's not the oxymoron it appears to be! Falling asleep after an exhausting day is passive relaxation. Crashing out in front of a film only to wake up, dribble down your chin, as the credits roll, that's passive too.

Active relaxation is things like mindfulness, meditation, masturbation, a simple yoga flow, reading, having a bath, going for an easy walk. It's being fully present in the moment you're in, not worrying about things that have already happened or are yet to happen. Through mindfulness, I have become so much better connected with my environment - appreciating the sound of the waves hitting the beach or the breeze rustling through the trees.

Mindfulness and gratitude go hand in hand. Once we start looking for positives, we start noticing them everywhere and they start to outnumber our negative thoughts, changing our mindset completely. It works for other things too, just look for what you want to see more of. Do you need to believe there's kindness in the world? Notice when you see someone being kind to someone else, or when you are kind to someone. Do you want to be a more creative or healthy person? Take time at the end of the day to reflect on the creative or healthy things you did that day.

Whatever worries we have about the past or future don't matter right now, they have already had or will have their own "now" someday. The present here-and-now moment is the only one that matters. And that present moment likely isn't as bad as you think, once you get your past and future stresses out of your head.

Last year, my husband and I found ourselves stuck in a traffic jam. What should have been a two hour drive to the airport for his birthday weekend away in Amsterdam ended up taking four, and that meant we missed our flight. That would be bad enough for anyone, but Steve has suffered with severe anxiety specifically rooted around being stuck in traffic, so it could have been a really difficult day.

I helped mindfully ground him in the moment, firstly by taking some deep breaths and then by encouraging him to think about all five senses right there and then – what could he see, smell, taste, hear, touch?

Sure, he could see lots of cars and angry people, but he could also see people jovially chatting between cars or rolling their eyes at the situation, he could see cows in the green fields and clouds in the blue sky as well as the cars in front and behind.

Next, I asked him what he was grateful for about our situation. After initially looking at me like I'd lost the plot (not entirely unreasonable), he was able to reel off a whole host of things.

He was grateful the sun was shining, that we were warm and safe, that we had snacks and drinks, that we were comfortable. He was grateful to be facing this situation with me, whom he felt safe with, and not with anyone else. He was grateful we didn't have our children with us, getting impatient and arguing with each other. He was grateful that we could afford to get an airport hotel for the night and get new flights the next morning, something which wouldn't have been true a year earlier (and still felt pretty extravagant).

Mindfulness and gratitude are such simple and life changing practices. As with being polite, they cost us nothing and can lift our day and mood so easily. But they can take real practice and dedication to get right.

If you find these practices difficult, a good way to start is to point out positive, beautiful things that you see in your day. It's all too easy to remember the one bad thing that happened and forget all the good things, so this practice better secures them in your memory. It's not about being grateful to God or anyone specific - if this feels difficult, thinking of it as appreciation rather than gratitude may help.

Every time you see a rainbow, stop and appreciate it, or send a photo of it to someone. When the barista makes you the most perfect coffee ever, be sure to thank them for it. When you find a beautiful shell or leaf, take a moment to consider what drew you to it.

I love walking and being out in the countryside, particularly the coast path. Whilst I do notice and appreciate the sea, the trees, the fields, the changing rocks and soil, birds, flowers, I tend to keep moving through nature rather than just being in it.

Since Oscar started home education, we've been volunteering together at a local forest school. It's taught me to get off of the path and just be in the trees, whatever the weather, appreciating and noticing the changing seasons. Sitting still in nature, listening to the birds and the wind in the trees; watching the squirrels; feeling the crunchy leaves underfoot or the shiny smooth green leaves and rough bark on the trees – it's so calming and really grounds me.

The more you start noticing the good things around you, the more your brain will learn to remember them and pay less attention to the less positive, more difficult things. This will make relaxation and mindfulness much easier, and that will impact the main type of rest that we need: sleep.

So many people I know talk about not sleeping for long enough or well enough. Not getting enough sleep impacts EVERYTHING. It makes you grumpy, unable to problem solve effectively, slower, more likely to comfort eat...

When my children were babies, sleep was the main topic of conversation between us parents. Some, like me, were struggling. Others were giving tips, sharing empathy and advice based on what had worked for them. A small, horrible, evil minority were bragging about how well their perfect angel baby slept through the night from three months old. (I still haven't forgiven those people.)

When I used to work full time in a juice bar, I was on my

feet all day and hauling around boxes of fruit in a (relatively!) physical job. My body would be tired at the end of the day, but my brain would be raring to go. In more mentally challenging sedentary office–based roles I had the opposite problem – my brain needed sleep but my body wanted to move. Finding the right balance between physical and mental work is important. As is getting outside in natural daylight as early as possible in the day, keeping your circadian rhythms in check. Could you get natural sunlight before you get any screenlight? (Note that if you use your phone as an alarm, this is guaranteeing the first thing you touch in the morning is your phone, making sunlight before screenlight almost impossible.)

These days I sleep really well. So well in fact that I often feel embarrassed and ashamed about it. A friend will admit to me that she goes to bed at nine, I tell her I do the same. She sighs with relief and starts telling me how great it is now getting up at five every day, going for sunrise runs... she's lost me. Morning snuggles are what make life worth living. I'll give them up for the occasional sunrise, but I usually get back into bed afterwards. I tell someone else that I go to bed at nine, and they congratulate me on how much I must get done around the house in the day. Erm, no, it just doesn't get done, it can wait 'til tomorrow. I prioritise my sleep over most other things, especially housework. People think I'm a party animal, not realising I always, always have a disco nap first. My game is to arrive early, get the party started, then slope off before midnight. (Just call me Cinderella.)

There are endless sleep tips out there: lavender pillow sprays, chilled eye masks, yoga nidra, white noise, turn your screens off, charge your phone in a different room...

My sleep tip is simple: Prioritise it. Sleep is more important than housework or exercise. Get eight to nine hours of sleep a night and your whole life will feel easier. If it's dark, you should be asleep (otherwise we'd be able to see in the dark!). That might mean that you live more seasonally – going into more of a hibernation mode in winter and being up and more active in summer.

With better sleep, you'll be able to face any challenge head on, be able to think more positively and more easily find solutions where you used to only see problems.

Rest Easy

What are your main takeaways from the previous chapter? How do you actively rest? How can you be more purposeful and better prioritise rest?

Play

Again, please take some time to think about how you play.

What do you do for fun? What does play mean to you? How did you like to play when you were a child? How often do you play? If you had a whole weekend with nothing to do and nowhere to be, how would you spend it?

Play Hard

The common theme across almost all of my coaching has been that people want to make more time for fun, joy, play, and creativity. They miss it and don't know how to get it back.

I anticipated that this would be an unexpected outcome, not something they would specifically seek out. I thought that once we'd worked on their burnout, grief, stress, procrastination, confidence, boundaries and whatever else was holding them back, they'd be pleasantly surprised that they were having more fun. Instead, it comes up early on, usually in our first session. Once they find more fun, they feel happier, calmer, and more productive. Crucially, they feel like they've found their own identity as an individual again, which may have been lost or hidden behind being a parent, partner, employee, or carer, or changed by parenthood, redundancy or bereavement.

In Catherine Price's book, The Power of Fun, she says that the recipe for True Fun is play plus flow plus connection. More often than not, the times when we are having fun are spent with other people, rather than by ourselves. The key to being open to that, is in feeling that you are already happy, that you have enough happiness to share with others – rather than hoping that others will fill your happy tank (though they likely will do that too). Do things from love, not for love.

If you haven't come across the term before, flow, or being "in the zone," is the state where you find yourself completely immersed in an activity; when time disappears and nothing else matters. Though you may be doing something that requires great skill and concentration, it feels effortless. Flow has even been described as "the secret to happiness." High praise indeed!

Flow is often associated with creative activities such as drawing, painting, playing an instrument, singing, dancing, cooking, knitting, and can often be reached through exercises like running, yoga, gymnastics, and other sports, and even driving, or playing chess. During flow, your mind is focused on the experience you are having rather than yourself or anything outside of that experience or moment.

On a playwork course I attended recently, we paired up and shared a favourite memory of playing as a child. There were common themes across all of our memories: they were outdoors, with other children, unsupervised, and with an element of risk involved (either direct physical danger like climbing a tree, or a risk that of being told off like going too far from home or sneaking into that abandoned haunted house). How often do our children get to do those sorts of activities now? Certainly not as much as we did, and even when they do, they are usually supervised and risk assessed.

As adults, we might have the occasional stag or hen party where we do a "risky" outdoor activity with friends, like coasteering or paintballing, but mostly they are organised and supervised (and not to mention expensive!). We might face risk at work sometimes, but I'm not sure we'd describe it as fun or play!

Play should be the most natural thing in the world. Even animals who are struggling for the survival of their species can be seen playing when they're not hunting, eating, or resting. Too often we humans can see play as a waste of time when there is so much work to be done, more money to be earned, someone to impress to get that promotion, DIY and cleaning to do. Creativity can be lost altogether because we don't think we're good enough – it becomes about the end product and not the process of creating it.

Go and find a piece of paper and a pen. I want you to have a go at drawing your partner or friend, with them sitting in front of you. You're going to give them the picture afterwards to keep.

How do you feel?

Nervous?

Will you draw the picture?

I'm not sure I would – maybe just a smiley face or a stick figure.

Now, put the paper on top of your head and do the drawing.

Feel better?

With the pressure of creating a "good" picture removed, you can have fun drawing. You know the end result will look messy and probably nothing like your subject. You can enjoy having a go and laughing at the end result.

Creativity should first be about messing around, getting ideas down even if it's obvious they won't work. Think of the ideas stage as the accelerator. Too often we can slam on the brakes by critiquing our (or other people's) ideas too soon, giving suggestions for improvements. You can't accelerate and brake at once – accelerate first, get your ideas out (even if they're ridiculous) and then come back to develop them with fresh eyes, using your creative brake to edit and slow down.

As the oldest sibling in a single parent household, when I was a child I loved taking on responsibility and being a grown up before my time. I loved working hard at school and mainly played imaginative adventurous games, on my own. I loved to read, and I hated (I mean, I really, really HATED) sports. As soon as I started high school, I stopped doing PE. I just didn't turn up for the lessons, preferring to go home and enjoy a couple of blissful hours of the house to myself instead.

Once we are out of childhood, play generally means sports or music. Sport was clearly out of the question for me, and, after years of violin lessons with zero progress, so was music.

I'd tried joining a junior rowing team when I was about ten, only to be unceremoniously booted off of it for not being good enough to race. So when I made friends with a group of mums after Oscar was born, and they all started their own rowing team, I never even considered joining. It was a hardwired limiting belief that I couldn't row. It was similarly hardwired that I couldn't run, or do exercise of any sort.

As a group of mums with small children, it quickly became apparent that exercising was generally the only way I could see my friends without babies in tow. So eventually, I gave in and started rowing and running. In 2019 our team won an annual rowing race down the river Dart, and I ran my first marathon, starting in a most unexpected thunderstorm in Nice and running all the way to Cannes (you wouldn't be far wrong in thinking that it was just a sneaky holiday really!).

As an adult, I read a lot about the theory of play and flow before I was able to really put it into practice for myself. I was far too busy working, parenting, trying to be a good wife, friend and daughter. The only way I really knew how to play was to get drunk and go dancing (life is infinitely better now that I know how to play sober too). I'd have tiny pockets of play where I'd switch off from life and be truly present with my children when they were small. But guilt-ridden thoughts of washing up or work, or just a feeling of boredom, would inevitably intrude and tear me away after a few minutes.

During my thirties, as my children became more independent, I started to discover my more playful self. I joined a hula hoop class, started experimenting in the kitchen more, and had a go at creative writing. I became more body confident, so sex became about play and flow too. When you have sex, are you truly there enjoying it? Or are you worrying about how you look or who might hear you or not wanting to make a mess or what you're going to make for dinner? (I often like to challenge my clients, especially mums, to stand naked in front of a full length mirror and list all the things they love about their body. As with practicing gratitude, if you start purposefully noticing the good things, you'll start to see them more easily and find the things you dislike easier to ignore or learn to love.)

Through play, I learned to completely relax and be in the moment. To love my job and give it my all and be able to leave it behind at the end of the day to go and enjoy myself – and to eat right and sleep properly so that I could go and give it my all again the next day.

I believe that everyone could benefit from playing more. My mission is to help people remove their personal barriers to play so they can lead a more joyful and fulfilling life that they look back on with no regrets.

My play hero is my dad. He taught me to work as little as possible: just enough that I had the time and money to play hard.

He was always out adventuring: caving, abseiling, diving, rock climbing, and generally exploring and having a good time. Now in his seventies, his flat is full of science toys and flashing lights, he's always experimenting in the kitchen (often exploding things in the microwave), and the vast majority of his time is spent play fighting with his dog.

He'd spend a couple of weeks earning a few grand (he had innovative solutions to fixing swimming pools which could've made him a fortune if he'd chosen work over play) and then use that to fund six months travelling.

It didn't make him the best dad in the world, don't get me wrong. He could've stayed in the UK working and contributing to our family; physically, financially and emotionally.

But I'd rather have him away and happy, than at home miserable and bringing us all down with him. He wasn't meant to be held down and I don't think he could ever have been happy with a traditional life.

Mum dying in her fifties showed me that life is too short not enjoy it; that we have to squeeze every ounce of experience out of life that we can. Dad's way of life showed me that it's possible to do that. We can't follow anyone else's dreams and expectations and expect to find happiness or fulfillment.

As a single parent to my brother and me, Mum had less time for play, but she was brilliant at creating play opportunities with and for us. For her, play was more likely going for a hike and getting lost and muddy somewhere, usually in the rain.

I have many fond memories of one of her friends visiting sporadically. They'd been at primary school together many years earlier. Once, the music teacher asked the two of them to, "Go and get in the cupboard." She wanted the portable cupboard full of instruments brought into the room.

They took the instruction literally and were found sat in the cupboard with all the instruments out on the floor outside where they'd had to make room to get in.

Forty years later, they would still be in absolute stitches laughing about this every time they got together. The kind of laugh that you can only have with someone you feel completely safe with. The kind that becomes noiseless, hurts your tummy, and leaves your eyes streaming. The kind where, even once it's over and you've finally got your breath back, you only need to look at each other for a second to start up again.

If that pure, unbridled laughter isn't the best kind of flow, then I don't know what is!

Personally, I find flow most easily through cooking whilst singing along to loud music, but through lockdown I tried working on finding my flow in other ways – with varying levels of success! Embroidery, knitting, piano, drawing, painting, and yoga all kept me interested for a while but didn't fully grab my attention enough to get me to a good enough skill level that flow was even possible.

I love hula hooping, which is considered a "flow art" (all those things you see at festivals: poi, juggling, fire dancing). I love it because it's okay to be out of time, drop the hoop, and do it your own way. I can do it whilst watching TV or reading a book. I can do it in the lounge, in the garden, or on the beach. I don't need to wear trainers or a sports bra – but it does go very well with sparkly and colourful clothing! I can do it for five minutes or put on my favourite album and hoop for an hour. I've never been to an exercise class where I laugh so much or where the time goes so fast as a hoop class.

Roller discos and ice skating are great sources of playful flow for me too. The first few minutes are a bit wobbly and laughter-fuelled, and then I get the hang of it. I zoom around feeling like I'm floating, weaving in and out of other people and switching my mind off from thoughts of anything else.

This year, I've found flow in swimming too.

I'm not a swimmer. I'm bad with the cold. I have to hold my nose when I go under. My hair is too thick and unruly for any washing and drying that isn't absolutely necessary. I can't even do any proper strokes.

But switching swimming in my head to a play activity instead of a form of exercise has brought me so much joy, brought me so many lovely bonding opportunities with my boys, and better connected me with the sea and where I live.

Before I had children, I would occasionally go swimming and slowly plough up and down the pool in a constant state of boredom, just counting my lengths. When my children were little, I loved taking them swimming and playing in the water with them. Once they were big enough to swim safely on their own though, I avoided swimming as much as possible. It was a hassle getting everyone changed and having to wash my hair. I was happier sitting on the side of the pool with a book, or sending Steve to the pool so I could stay at home and keep out of it altogether.

Now though, I love swimming with my boys and playing with them in the pool again like when they were little. Swimming has become about fun again, not about fitness. Sometimes we go for a swim in the sea, screeching at the cold and jumping into the waves. In the pool, we have underwater running races instead of swimming lengths, and play fights with different imaginary weapons and rules. There is very little actual swimming involved. (It helps enormously that they can get themselves dressed now, too!)

Play doesn't have to be about doing an activity though. It can much smaller and simpler than that.

How many of these ideas could you tick off today to inject some play more into your day?

- Have a tickle fight with your kids;
- Pretend to be a rockstar when you're driving;
- Belly laugh over a bottle of wine with friends;
- Make a pile of Autumn leaves and jump into them;
- Dance manically round the kitchen while the kettle boils;
- Flash your partner to make them laugh when they're on an important phone call;
- Run as fast as you can, not to get fit, but because you want to feel the wind in your hair;
- Have the kind of sex that's definitely not about making a baby (with yourself counts too).

Play Easy

What are your main takeaways from the previous chapter? How do you like to play? How could you integrate more play into your life?

IV

The Result

Once you've put things in place to ensure that you have got the right balance of work, rest and play, how will your life be different? What "one day" goals will you be ready to start working towards and how will you go about it?

Dealing with Change

Change can be difficult, even when it's welcome and positive change.

You might be changing your life in a way that you've chosen, like moving house, having a baby, starting a new job or business, or retiring. Or life might be changing in a way you haven't chosen for yourself, like illness, bereavement, redundancy, or a break up.

Either way, you're likely to go through a grieving process of some description as you say goodbye to the life you had and felt safe and comfortable in to leap into an unknown and unfamiliar future.

Sometimes chosen changes can hit you the hardest, because you've been excited and motivated for your new life, so haven't stopped to think about what you'll be leaving behind. Changes that are outside of your control tend to garner more sympathy and support from people around you because it's expected and accepted that they are difficult.

Soon after my mum was diagnosed with terminal cancer, I had a meeting with a local GP about a new role we were taking on to support people at the end of their life and their carers. She explained to me that when a death was anticipated and talked about openly and honestly, a lot of the grieving process could happen whilst the person was still alive. This was such reassuring information to me after Mum's death, when I often felt like I was dealing with things "too well."

Growing up, we'd always talked openly about death in our family. As a single parent, Mum made sure we knew where to find all the relevant information we'd need in case she died: the green folder. We got to choose who we'd want to take us on if she died. (Lorraine was the easy choice. She looked like Princess Diana; had a super cool Volkswagen Beetle with a cat statue on the dashboard; had a swing and seesaw in her garden; and always, always had a packet of Polos, a pen, and plasters in her bag, as I firmly believed all proper mums should.)

So throughout her illness, Mum and I would talk quite openly about her mortality - more so the less imminent it felt. We planned her funeral (not knowing it would be subject to Covid restrictions when the time came), and she wrote cards for everyone she knew for me to give out after she died. Sometimes I felt that people thought I was morbid or pessimistic when I spoke about Mum's coming death in such a matter of fact way, but I just felt that I was being realistic and honest about what was happening, facing it head on.

One day at the start of Mum's cancer journey, I caught the train to Bristol for a Social Prescribing (that's where health professionals suggest lifestyle changes and connection through community activities instead of, or as well as, traditional medications and treatments) conference. I had a short walk in pouring February rain from the station to the venue. The weather accurately reflected my mood. I hadn't told anyone Mum's news yet, so was holding onto it myself - saying it out loud would make it real and I wasn't ready for that yet. A stranger stopped me in the street, in the rain, to compliment me on my outfit (a big bright swishy pleated skirt – not very practical on a rainy day!) and put a smile on my face that would completely turn my day around for the better.

I arrived at the conference feeling energised and motivated. I scrawled reams and reams of notes and ideas, excited to get back to work and share what I'd learned and start putting my learning into practice.

Then Tenofus choir provided some entertainment for the end of the conference. A woman of about my age stood shaking in front of the rest of the choir and told her story. Her mum had died of cancer, leading her to join this choir which was for people affected by cancer (i.e. pretty much anyone). She told her story, which left me with tears running down my face, and then the choir performed to finish the conference.

I met up with a couple of friends for a drink before catching my train home. I told them about Mum, the first people beside my husband that I had told. I felt nervous, in a similar way to when I was announcing that I was pregnant, but it was a relief to say it out loud at last. We ended up talking for so long that I missed my train.

Then, at the station as I waited for the next train, I bought myself another beer and sat quietly contemplating life, the universe and everything (and incidentally, remembering the wonderful biscuit story from So Long and Thanks for All the Fish, one of the four books in the Hitchhiker's Guide to the Galaxy Trilogy).

I missed the next train too.

That day accurately sums up what grieving has been like for me. Constantly and unpredictably changing from one emotion to the next without warning. Sad, defeated, lost, grateful, energised, motivated, quietly sobbing, happy to be with friends, wanting to be alone, thoughtful, melancholy, disorganised, laughing.

Early into the first lockdown, a friend of mine introduced me to The Grief Spiral model. Imagine a spider's web: a spiral with lines going out from the centre to the outside. Each of the straight lines represents an emotion: denial, anger, bargaining, depression, and acceptance being the standard stages of grief, but you can choose your own for this. You might feel panic, fear, confusion, shock, sadness, loneliness, for example.

You start in the centre of the spider's web and follow the spiral out. Each time you cross a straight line, you feel that emotion. So at first you're alternating between several different and strong emotions all the time with little relief. As time goes on, there are longer gaps between the strong emotions. Sometimes there's a trigger that brings it on, like an anniversary or going to a certain place or hearing a specific song. Other times it will take you completely by surprise. Whenever you feel those big emotions, they are as strong as ever, but they happen less frequently and you learn how to feel them and move on more quickly.

This model works for other kinds of change too. Let's say you're starting a business or writing a book. I can tell you from my very current personal experience that there's a similar but perhaps even more wildly oscillating pattern of emotions such as uncertainty, self belief, imposter syndrome, confidence, blind panic, excitement, nervousness, laziness, motivation. It really helps to notice these emotions, to accept them, and reflect on what they're trying to tell you.

Is that nervousness just there because you really care about what you're doing, or is it a sign that you need to do some additional research or preparation? How much is your confidence affected by external factors and how can you become more confident even without receiving external recognition?

So, whenever you embark on change, be sure to take the time to reflect on what you'll be leaving behind as well as what you'll be welcoming. There will likely be things you'll be glad to let go of or you wouldn't be making the change, but there will also be things you're sad to say goodbye to. Reflect on what those things are, and thank them for serving you in the past.

When working with clients who are experiencing a break up, bereavement, redundancy or any other kind of change they haven't chosen for themselves, I ask them what they're grateful for. Instead of focusing on what they've lost, what have they got from the experience that they can keep? How did they learn and grow in that relationship or job that has made their life better now than it would otherwise have been? What have they learned that might help them make good choices in future, set stronger clear boundaries, or recognise and avoid red flags? Then they can move towards their new goal with open arms, ready to welcome their new future.

What parts of your life would you like to say goodbye to, with gratitude for how they've served up you to now? What do you want to replace them with?

Saying Goodbye, with Gratitude

In Summer 2022, I was at a party and a bit bored. I went to get myself another drink to liven up a bit, only to realise: if I need alcohol to enjoy myself and feel comfortable here, do I really want to be here in the first place?

I tried to stop drinking from that point, but starting that in summer is really challenging and I kept finding myself with a drink in my hand. Next thing I knew, it was Christmas and the prosecco was in full flow.

Alcohol has never been a real problem for me. I love drinking and always have fun. I've never blacked out, or smashed up my phone, or lost my keys. I've only very occasionally felt the need to have a drink because I'm stressed out. I've racked up a fair few horrendous hangovers, but nothing I couldn't handle.

So my incentive wasn't strong. There was no "rock bottom" moment that showed me that I needed to stop once and for all.

But the idea kept niggling at me.

Several of my coaching clients casually dropped into conversation that they "don't really drink anymore" and they inspired me to finally give it a go. I wanted to be able to say that. It sounded casual and easy, very different to the phrase of someone who was "in recovery" or struggling to abstain.

I signed up to do an eight week mindfulness course and

decided to do the two things at the same time. That worked really well, doing the meditation and checking in with my mindfulness teacher each week helped keep me on track. I felt so healthy, glowing even!

My eight week goal became a one hundred day goal. And that's where I'm up to now as I write this in May 2023. I've done Dry January several times and not found it too difficult, but I also didn't feel any different than usual by the end of it, so the incentive to continue wasn't as strong as my desire to celebrate completing Dry January by, you guessed it, getting drunk.

After two months sober, and then three and beyond, I was feeling the benefits more and more. I've now lost the desire to drink again, and it feels permanent and even easy now that I'm not fighting myself.

I'm sleeping better and waking up full of energy and ideas and raring to go, so I'm more productive than ever. I feel healthier and that is evident in my skin; I've had so many comments about how much I'm glowing. I feel more confident than ever and like I'm getting to know the real me better. I just feel stupidly happy most of the time, wandering around with an inane grin on my face feeling grateful for everything. It makes me cringe to say it, but I really am "high on life."

To take on any new identity, we need to visualise it and believe it's possible. But to fully throw ourselves into our new identity, it's also important that we take the time to say goodbye to our old one.

So here's my break up letter to alcohol.

What do you need to say goodbye to from your past so that you're ready to greet your future with wide open arms?

Dear alcohol,

Thank you for giving me extra confidence when I needed it. Thank you for giving me an escape when life was hard. Thank you for helping me connect with people and have fun experiences without inhibition holding me back.

I'm grateful for all the things you've given me. I don't even begrudge the time you've stolen from me as I suffered from hangovers; they were worth it.

But I don't miss you and I don't need you anymore.

I'm confident enough without you now, even as I deal with stress or step outside of my comfort zone. I'm confident enough to turn down invitations to events where I feel I need alcohol to get through, or to leave when I'm not having a good time. I know I won't suffer from terrible FOMO anymore.

Maybe we'll still hang out sometimes. There's no hard feelings here from me. I just don't want or need you right now. I hope we can still be friends.

Thanks for all the good times,

Sunshine warm sober Chloe x

Goal Setting

I strive to experience joy and pleasure as much as possible. But I've learned that we shouldn't aim to feel joy all the time. If we feel something too often, it becomes normal and loses its spark. We need to feel those more difficult, less enjoyable emotions too, so that we can fully appreciate the more fun and fulfilling ones. Can we really know the full extent of pleasure if we haven't also experienced pain? The greater the potential risk, the greater the potential reward. We need a healthy balance of pain, peace and pleasure.

I hope that by applying some of the things I have suggested in this book, you will learn true contentment. You'll be happy with your life, not constantly smiling and laughing and having the greatest time ever, but enjoying and appreciating life for what it is – including the hard bits. Those more difficult things serve to make us stronger; they teach us and help us grow and develop. We all need them. Lean into them, embrace them, and find out what you can learn from them.

When something really hard is happening in your life, take a moment to consider what you can be grateful for about that thing. Whatever it is, there will always be something.

Once you've created better boundaries and got the balance right between work, rest, and play, life will feel more enjoyable and manageable. You will be able to find time for your hobbies, friends, and to start setting yourself goals that stretch you outside of your comfort zone so that you can design and create the life you've dreamed of, instead of living by default.

I blindly followed the path of sending my children to mainstream school because that's what everyone else did. We are hardwired to want to belong, and to be seen as normal. It can be hard to take your own path and do things your own way, but the rewards of living more authentically will surely be more fulfilling and therefore worth it.

For weeks - or more likely, months or even years - Oscar would tell me he wished he didn't have to go to school.

"Me too," I'd tell him, and I meant it.

After such a hard line on attendance, with the threat of fines if your child didn't attend school enough, I really didn't understand that it was a choice. I was asking school for help and understanding about his situation but my requests for help went unanswered, until we started receiving letters threatening court action for his poor attendance. By then he'd obviously made a big enough dent in their statistics that they felt duty bound to help him.

As soon as someone told me that home education was in fact a choice, I made that choice. And it's a choice for Charlie too. He can choose to go to school or he can choose home education. For now, he chooses school, because he loves the socialising and he wants to be stretched and challenged. Knowing that it's a choice, an investment, that he continues to make even when he's having a hard day, makes a huge difference compared to the feeling of having no other option.

My children both have different talents. So I use different approaches to suit each of them. I put them in different environments to suit their individual needs. And they each work towards different goals that are interesting, stretchy and challenging for them. They focus on their own goals and journey rather than comparing themselves to each other or anyone else, because comparison is the thief of joy.

I was brought up vegetarian from birth. Being a vegetarian child in the eighties and nineties was really difficult at times. My friends' parents didn't know what to feed me, and school dinners and vegetarian options in restaurants couldn't always be trusted. (I remember once being given a school dinner that was clearly fish, complete with bones - I'm still baffled that some people think that fish aren't animals or that they don't feel pain!) People loved to taunt me with bacon, and I am still unable to eat in the dark for fear that someone will slip some onto my plate thinking it's funny. It was a hard choice for Mum to make, but she was doing what she believed in: it's not okay to kill animals for food when there are plenty of plants to go around.

In my thirties, I discovered that the dairy industry is even more cruel than the meat industry, and began my vegan-ish journey (I never aim for perfection. It is the enemy of good! Aim for gold and you'll be disappointed with silver - aim for bronze and you'll be thrilled with silver!). I met my now good friend Dr Alan Desmond and went home with a new identity. Walking home that night, my husband messaged me asking me to pick up some milk, to which I replied, "We don't drink milk anymore."

No longer was I trying my best to go vegan or to cut out dairy, or challenging myself to go vegan for a week or a month; I just didn't really have dairy anymore. That simple identity shift made the change to a mostly plant-based diet infinitely easier for me.

Mum, and others like her, helped to pave the way for the plant-based movement that is happening now, where there are vegan options on most menus and a huge range of vegan alternatives available in mainstream supermarkets.

I include this here, because veganism is one of the best examples to explain why understanding the purpose behind a goal is so important. Some people are vegan for animal welfare reasons. Others for health reasons. Others for environmental reasons. If your reason is animal welfare, then you might be okay with eating a diet of mainly chips and bread and vegan ice cream. If you're in it for your health, you will likely choose whole (unprocessed) foods. And if it's about climate change for you, you might choose to only eat food that is grown locally - or you might even choose to add insects to your diet!

The same goes for any goal. You need to know what you want to get from achieving your goal. If you're running a marathon, is your main motivation that you want to get fitter, beat a previous time, raise money for charity, make friends in a running community, travel somewhere new, lose weight, or to show yourself you can do it? If you're writing a book, is it because you want fame and fortune, or to help people, or to challenge yourself? Knowing your purpose is what will keep you on track when it gets difficult - which it inevitably will if you're stretching yourself outside of your comfort zone.

Veganism also serves to show an example of push and pull factors in our goal setting. Choosing veganism because you care about animals, health, and the planet is brilliant. They're all pushing you away from eating meat and dairy. Having good pull factors as well will make your life much easier though. That means focusing on all the delicious foods you can have, all the new things you want to try, feeling more body confident, or having more energy. Those things are much more motivating and will make you more likely to succeed, as will giving yourself permission to not be perfect.

If there's something you'd like to do that goes against the norm, goal setting is going to be an important part of your development. Sharing your journey can feel vulnerable, but it can help others who are considering making similar changes, and it can help you feel more accountable and more likely to follow through on your goals.

Goal setting is a huge part of coaching. Without setting goals that stretch you outside of your comfort zone and towards a better future, you can't expect to grow and develop the way you want to. Understanding your values, beliefs and emotions helps you to set goals that are right for you and to find ways to overcome any barriers that might get in your way.

Learning these skills through coaching has led me to do things like run a marathon, write a book, start a business, take Oscar out of school, and so much more that I might not otherwise have even attempted.

Goal setting has really helped me in home educating Oscar too. We might set a goal for the term that we stick to, but the ways in which we reach that goal might change as we follow his interests. For example, last Autumn term his goal was to make a Christmas gift for his Forest School leaders to show his gratitude to them. It could have been anything. In the end, he designed a birdhouse (involving research into ideal sizes and positioning as well as maths and technical drawing skills) and then made it with the help of his grandad (woodwork and communication skills, as well as risk assessment and safety). He also wrote a lovely story to go with his gift (storytelling, spellings, grammar, editing, even a little map reading and research about birds and trees). He could equally have chosen to buy them a box of chocolates or baked them a cake and still achieved his goal.

I've always been very future focused. As a child, when one birthday party came to an end, Mum would still be cleaning up as I was already telling her what I wanted to do for my party the next year. I never took a moment to just enjoy having just had a lovely party with all my friends, just as many of my clients don't pause to celebrate achieving one goal before moving straight onto the next. (Though they will dwell on the thing that went wrong for plenty of time!)

My future focused goal setting nature came partly from Mum. Back in the early nineties, she was a single mum taking on whatever work she could get. She was a barmaid, a receptionist, a cleaner, a dinner lady, and a classroom assistant. The way she used to tell the story, she had visions of a gravestone engraved with the words, "Here lies unfulfilled potential."

After some gentle encouragement from the school head-teacher and my stepdad, Mum went to university, aged thirty-four, to train to be a teacher.

Soon after she qualified, I was visiting my old primary school. The headteacher who had got Mum started in the first place approached me to tell me they had a teaching vacancy, and that Mum should apply.

She almost didn't do it. She still didn't believe in herself.

With some more encouragement from my stepdad, she went for the job.

Although I was only young, I still vividly remember the evening after the interview as she waited by the phone. As time went on, she became more and more convinced that she couldn't have got the job because they would have contacted the successful candidate first. But then the call came and of course they offered her the job!

In fact, she stayed at the school for twenty years. Not only did she fulfill her own potential, she inspired and motivated hundreds of pupils to fulfill theirs too. After a childhood full of hairy experiences (think getting snowed in on Dartmoor or stranded by the tide on a beach or stuck deep in a cave with only one working light between four of us) she told me were, "character building," Mum even went on to specialise in character education.

So after spending my teenage years watching Mum become a teacher and meet her goals, I felt that my own higher purpose in life was to help people reach their full potential. I was lucky enough to find employment that allowed me to do that from the age of nineteen. I was generally working alongside older colleagues who had left high paying corporate careers to go and "give something back."

I've always worked in jobs that were focused on helping people to set and achieve goals that would get them from where they were to where they wanted to be. At the start of my career, I helped people with disabilities to find work experience as a stepping stone towards sustainable employment. Then I supported people to come off of benefits by starting their own small businesses. And in my charity work, I matched volunteers with lonely elderly people to help both feel more connected. All of these roles inspired me by introducing me to people who were determined to improve their lives even when they faced additional challenges and hurdles.

I have often reflected on whether it's better to help a few people a lot, or a lot of people a little bit. I hope that this book will help me help a lot of people a little bit, whilst through my coaching I can help a few people a lot.

In more recent years, particularly seeing how important gratitude and mindfulness were in keeping Mum smiling even as she was dying of cancer, I've realised that my purpose is more about helping people appreciate the present – learning to want what you already have, rather than always striving for more.

The future is important, but sometimes we can be so focused on it that we miss out on the joy we could be experiencing right now. When you think about getting to the end of your endless to do list, finishing all the DIY in your house, or retiring, what do you imagine yourself doing? Could you be doing more of that right now?

Because that magical future never comes.

Once you're there, it's just another "now."

Many people finally reach their goals only to feel disappointed, because life isn't suddenly and magically perfect. They need something to strive for, so immediately set themselves another goal and start working towards it without a pause to celebrate their current achievement.

Let's take, "I want to be mortgage free before I'm fifty," as an example goal. Initially you might say that's unrealistic, you can't afford to do that. But what are your options? You could take on another job or more overtime to increase your income. You could forgo holidays and nights out to decrease your outgoings. You could move to a smaller house or a different area to have a smaller mortgage. You could get a lodger. You could rent your house out and rent somewhere cheaper for yourself.

There are always options. You just need to decide how important your goal is to you. What would being mortgage free by fifty mean for you? Perhaps that you could work less, retire earlier, afford more holidays, or feel more secure. And what would it cost you? Maybe time with your family, holidays and treats right now, and your health as you'll likely be more stressed by working hard and having to meet higher monthly payments.

So would mortgage free by fifty-five or sixty be a more realistic goal that would still stretch you whilst allowing you to enjoy your life more right now? Or maybe you want to make the goal even more challenging, to be mortgage free by forty-five?

All we have is the moment we are in. We need to learn to better appreciate and accept it for what it is. If we learn to make the most of the present, we can trust that the future will take care of itself. It's time to surrender and enjoy the journey, rather than spend our lives waiting for the destination.

So now when I'm setting goals - for myself or with others - I use manifesting techniques to bring those goals into the present tense. I encourage my clients to start with a goal that includes a "by" (timescale) and a "why" (purpose).

Then we get manifesting.

Manifesting. It's a bit of a dirty word, I know.

That's where you just picture what you want and then wait and it comes to you, right? Sounds a bit fishy.

I'm afraid that, as with most things, if it sounds too good to be true, it probably is.

But having now learned more about manifesting, I realise how much sense it makes. This is how it works for me.

What would you do if someone from the future could come back and tell you it would all work out? If you had no fear whatsoever, just absolute faith. What would you do if you had time, if money were no object, and if you weren't worried what others might think of you?

91

That's essentially what manifesting is all about: knowing what you want and really believing it's totally possible and going to happen, so that going for it doesn't feel risky or scary or hard anymore. As my son, Oscar succinctly puts it, "Say what you want, as if you already have it."

He got me with that one in the summer, when he shouted from the sea: "I'm having fun playing in the waves with my mum!"

I couldn't not join him after that, no matter how warm I was on the beach and how cold I knew I'd be in the sea!

Think of a time when something didn't go the way you planned. What was the learning or silver lining from it going wrong? In hindsight, are you glad things went the way they did? What are you grateful for about that experience? (The message here is: even if your manifesting doesn't work out the way you want, it'll probably be okay anyway, so you might as well surrender to it and give it a go!)

If you can't even picture your dreams, it's much harder to make them a reality. Take the time to visualise having everything you want, achieving all your goals. Imagine it in your head, draw a picture, make a collage or mood board, write it down, tell a friend – whatever works for you. What does it look like? What can you hear, smell, taste, and touch? What emotions come up for you as you imagine your dream future life where everything turns out just as you hope it will? What advice would your future self, the one who has already achieved the goal, give you?

What would achieving those goals and having the things you want give you? Maybe your initial answer is more money, a bigger house, more holidays. Keep asking what that would give you long enough and you'll come up with an answer like happiness or security or connection.

Now try saying aloud that you already have that thing: "I am happy." Can you say it and believe it? If not, what needs to change for it to become true?

Recently I worked with a client who was a single mum. She wasn't happy renting the house she was in; it felt like a step backwards from being a homeowner, as she'd been when she was married, and before that. Buying a house wasn't realistic, though it's still her long-term goal. As we delved deeper into her goal, she told me that buying a house would help her feel more settled. It would feel like her permanent home, not just a house she lived in temporarily. So I asked what it would take for her to feel more settled in the house she was renting, and for it to feel more permanent.

A week later, she told me that she'd got permission from her landlord to paint some walls and had started it already, and she'd finally unpacked those last remaining boxes. Hopefully she'll still get to buy her own house again one day. In the meantime, she's already feeling more settled where she is, and she can enjoy being there without feeling like it's not "enough."

If you believe you've already got what you want, you can stop wanting it. It becomes easier to surrender to life and accept things as they are.

I fully understood this as I launched my coaching business. If I was meeting a potential client and I felt uneasy about charging them, I'd likely end up offering them coaching for free or underselling myself. But if I went into that meeting believing that I was a good coach and that people paid me for my work and that they got good value for money, then I would be more confident in the meeting and charge what I was worth. I applied this approach even before I'd got my first paying client, and I believe it's a big part of why I got that first one!

It's one way to get rid of imposter syndrome and perfection-ism too. If you truly believe that you are good enough, then you will act good enough. Others will see that and believe in you too, and before you know it, it will be true.

Fake it 'til you make it.

Dress for the job you want, not the one you have.

Believe in yourself and trust that the rest will follow.

What would your manifestation be?

Your goal, stated in the present tense, that you can already confidently say and believe it's true. The opposite of that belief that's been holding you back.

"I have a beautiful family home that is big enough for all our needs."

"I run a successful business and have a great work-life balance."

It might simply be a feeling, like "I am content," or an identity, like "I am a healthy person," or "I am a marathon runner."

Your Goals

What goals are you working towards? What will achieving them mean for you?

V

The Hopscotch Method

When you have a goal in mind, work your way through the questions on an imaginary (or get out the chalk and do it for real!) hopscotch to really help you visualise achieving it and the steps you'll need to take to do so. For best results, ask a friend to read the questions out to you and make some notes. By the end of this, you will be able to present your goal as a manifestation and have far more belief and motivation to achieve it.

Hop, Skip, Jump!

Throughout my training as a coach, I resisted using models. I didn't think it would feel very professional to pull out a script in the middle of a session - certainly none of the coaches I'd worked with had ever done so.

Then, towards the end of my training, I was introduced to Robert Dilts' Logical Levels of Change model, from the field of Neuro-Linguistic Programming. We were paired up to practice using the model with a fellow trainee coach. I'll admit, I wasn't excited to use it. There was a long list of questions, all of which had to be asked in a certain order and in a specific way. It went against the grain for me, to say the least.

As I asked my partner, Jos, the questions, and had her standing up and moving around her office, it all just clicked. This was the model for me! I could picture asking these questions, with a few adjustments to suit my personal style, and using hopscotch imagery to add a more playful element to it.

To use this model yourself, you will need to stand and have a small area to move around in. You can of course consider these questions seated if you prefer, but it won't have the same impact. Imagine hopscotch is drawn out in front of you, from one to ten. (Even better, if you can get outside, why not go and find some chalk and actually draw it!)

You will be making your way from one to ten thinking about all the things you will need to do on the journey to achieving your goal. Then, you'll be making your way back from ten to one imagining that you have already achieved it.

I have had incredible results using this model, the act of moving through time and visualising achieving your goal is very powerful.

By the end of the model, your goal will be a fully formed manifestation and you'll feel more confident and ready to go get it!

I've included my own brief answers for writing this book for you to see an example.

1: Your Goal

So, we start at number one, where you state your goal, as a positive. Avoid any hint of saying what you don't want to do or what you want to do less of. And be sure that the "I want" part is true too. This should be something you really want, not something you think you should want or that someone else has suggested. Remember to include a "by" and a "why" in your goal.

I want to write and self publish a book by summer 2023 so that I can help more people.

2: When and Where

Move to number two, and think about when and where you will achieve your goal. How will you know the moment that you have achieved it? Is your timescale realistic? What season will it be? What will the weather be like? Will it be a certain time of day? What will you be wearing? Who else will be there?

It will be a warm summer day when I'm sat in my office by myself submitting my final manuscript for publication.

3: Celebrations

On number three, it's time to think about celebrating achieving your goal. Where will you be? Who will you be with? What will you be wearing? How will you celebrate? What can you see, hear, taste, smell? Can you picture the moment or sharing your joy at achieving something that is important to you?

I will celebrate on my trip to watch Pulp live on their reunion tour.

4: Behaviour

Making your way to number four, it's time to think about how you will need to behave to achieve your goal. Do you need to stick to a strict training schedule, go to bed earlier, eat right, or set better boundaries for yourself?

I will post consistently on social media to build anticipation so people want to order my book as soon as they can.

5: Plan

Now on number five, think about your plan. What actions do you need to take? Are you clear on the steps and order of them? What will happen if you do nothing? What do you need to do first? What milestones lie ahead of you between now and achieving your goal?

I need to finish editing, get it proof read, typeset, design the cover, and market it.

6: Confidence

Number six is all about your confidence. How would you rate your confidence to achieve this goal, within your desired timescale, from one to ten? What could you do to improve that rating?

I am 10/10 confident that I will release my book this summer.

7: Values

On number seven, you'll be thinking about your values and how this goal will honour them. What's really important to you? How will achieving this goal meet your values?

My values are freedom, balance, connection, sharing, community. My book shares some of my ways to find freedom, balance, and connection with my community.

8: Beliefs

Now moving onto number eight, consider the positive beliefs you will need to hold as you work toward your goal. What limiting beliefs, fears, or assumptions do you need to challenge so that you can believe in yourself and your ability to achieve your goal?

I will need to believe that I've got something to say that people want to hear, and that I'm a good enough writer that people will enjoy reading it.

9: Identity

Number nine is all about your identity. Who do you want and need to be to do this? A healthy person, a determined person, a confident person, or a generous person? A runner, a writer, a reader, a coach, a student, an educator, an entrepreneur, or a parent? What role models do you look up to and what can you learn from them?

I will be a writer and a coach who leads by example by setting and achieving my own goals which stretch me outside of my comfort zone.

10: Higher Purpose

Now you've made it up to number ten, ask yourself how this goal honours your higher purpose, the legacy that you want to leave the world. How is this goal relevant to your whole life and how you want to be seen and remembered by others?

I want to help other people be happier and healthier, to live authentic and fulfilling lives.

10: Looking Back

Phew! Turn around and look back at where you came from. Imagine that you have just achieved and celebrated your goal. How does it feel? What advice would your future self give you now as you embark on your journey toward this goal?

Keep at it and you'll be able to help more lots of people a little bit through your book, and more people a lot because they'll find you as a coach because of your book. You've got this!

9: Identity

Take a step back to number nine and ask yourself, who are you, now that you have achieved that goal? Say it, out loud, and in the present tense. How does that feel? Do you believe yourself?

I am a writer and a coach.

8: Beliefs

On number eight, what positive beliefs do you hold about yourself now that you have achieved your goal? (Some of the phrases you come up with here will make great affirmations for days when things aren't going to plan – be sure to write them down.)

My ideas, experiences, and questions help other people to help themselves and improve their lives.

7: Values

Back on number seven, how have you honoured your values by achieving your goal? How are you continuing to honour them every day?

I am sharing things that will help people be happier and healthier and reaching as many people as I can.

6: Confidence

Number six: now that you've achieved this goal, how confident are you about stretching yourself and achieving future goals?

10/10 – I can do anything!

5: Plan

Onto number five, it's time to review your plan of action. Did the advice of your future self show you that anything needs to change from your original plan?

Make a proper marketing plan.

4: Behaviour

As you move to number four, think about how you had to behave to achieve your goal. Which behaviours will continue even after you have achieved and celebrated your goal?

I write every day – in my journal, on social media, or for a future project.

3: Celebrations

This is the fun one! How did you celebrate achieving your goal? Where were you, who with? What did you do? What did you eat or drink? Who else was there? What do you need to do to make it a reality?

I will book myself a haircut and treat myself to a new dress for seeing Pulp.

2: When and where

Almost there now! On number two, when did you actually achieve the goal? Where were you? Does your original timescale still seem reasonable?

I will make my launch date 04/07/23 – the third anniversary of Mum dying, which feels right since I know she'd be proud of me doing this, and a week before Pulp.

1: Your Goal

Finally back to number one, it's time to state your goal again, in the present tense, as though you've already achieved it: a manifestation. How does that feel, compared to when you stated the goal at the start of the exercise? What have you learned?

I am inspiring, motivating and empowering people to create a happier balance in their lives through my coaching, social media posts, and book.

Journal template

There's no right or wrong way to journal, but here are some ideas to help you get started.

A common method of journaling is "Morning Pages" in which you write two or three pages first thing every morning. There is no aim to these, you might write absolute rubbish. It's a warm up to help you empty your head of thoughts and get your creative juices flowing. By doing it first thing in the morning, you are prevented from overthinking it and trying to write something interesting, funny or beautiful.

You can replicate this same method any time of day of course, and just get writing. Let your brain switch off and your hand take over. Give it a try, you might be surprised what comes out.

You might choose to journal in other ways too. Maybe you would prefer to do something more visual like a mindmap or drawing, or write in bullet points, or say your thoughts out loud even if only to yourself.

There's something really powerful about getting those thoughts out of your head and freeing up space to start finding solutions to your problems and acting on your ideas.

In Rest Hard, I described the format I used for my daily journaling during lockdown. On the following pages I give an example template for you to use each morning or evening to get you started. You might choose to split your goals and gratitude so that you have one each for work, rest and play.

Daily Journal Template (Morning)

How did I get on with my goals yesterday?

1

2

3

What happened yesterday?

What am I feeling stressed or worried about?

What am I looking forward to?

What are my goals for today?

1

2

3

What am I feeling grateful for?

1

2

3

What else do I want to say?

Daily Journal Template (Evening)

How did I get on with my goals today?

1

2

3

What happened today?

What am I feeling stressed or worried about?

What am I looking forward to?

What are my goals for tomorrow?

1

2

3

What am I feeling grateful for?

1

2

3

What else do I want to say?

Acknowledgments

Thank you for reading my book! I hope it has helped you. I would really appreciate it if you could leave me a review on Amazon and let other people know about this book to help me spread my message further.

I'd never tried writing before the pandemic; but being stuck in my house for months on end forced me to try several new hobbies and writing was the one that stuck. So, I'm grateful to the lockdown for giving me the time to try something new, and grateful to the act of writing itself for how much it helped my mental health through such a difficult time.

You should probably be grateful too, because you're reading this instead of trying to smile at the poorly knitted jumper I made you or terrible song I tried to play you on the piano.

Thank you to my amazing, kind, loving husband Steve for being such a great support to me always and giving me all the freedom I need to play my way. Thank you to my favourite playmates, my beautiful children, Oscar and Charlie; I hope your lives will be abundant with love and joy.

Thank you to Amanda, who first introduced me to coaching. To Ana, Des and Jill for coaching me and showing me how it can help people achieve their dreams, confirming for me that it was the right path for me to take. To Jo and Zoe of In Good Company for training me up, and to Sophie for being my coach during the course. To Joanna Lott for helping me get my business off the ground. To Sally Singleton for teaching me to be a more mindful coach. And to NLP University for giving permission for me to use my adapted version of the Logical Levels of Change model.

A massive thank you to Debi for introducing me to the PAUSE, PLAY, CONNECT ® flow, and for volunteering to be one of my very first coaching clients to give me the chance to explore my skills and put the flow into practice.

To my hoop teacher Sophie, TRE teacher Jo, hairdressers Jenna and Sam, and beauty therapist Raphy who have all helped keep me sane over the last few years. Lockdown brought me an even stronger appreciation for all you do!

Thank you to my editor, April Grace O'Sullivan, and illustrator, Lars Flint, for bringing my book to life! And to Jacqueline who took me on as one of her practice clients and supported me through writing and sharing it.

To my friends: my school besties, The Mummies, The Seagulls, and all the rest of you. I'm so lucky to have so many friends and such a great community around me.

To my dad, who showed me that play matters and that I should live life by my own rules. To my stepdad Terry, who is always ready with a bad joke when you need one, and especially when you don't.

And finally, thank you to my mum. My act of teenage rebellion was to avoid any essay subjects you could have helped me with – I needed my independence! You always said that everyone had at least one book in them. You never got to finish yours. I hope you like mine!

About the Author

Chloe Myers lives by the sea in Devon, England with her husband and two sons. They lead an idyllic life full of all the joys of a typical British seaside holiday: long days at the beach, gorging on chips and ice creams and pasties, building sandcastles, playing on boats, paddling in the sea, jumping in the waves, and clambering over rocks.

Chloe's coaching career started at nineteen, supporting people with disabilities to find sustainable employment. After a decade in the Welfare to Work sector, she moved to the voluntary sector. Her initial role with Volunteering in Health was Volunteer Co-ordinator - recruiting mostly retired people to become volunteer befrienders and introducing them to lonely, isolated people to visit in their homes, so that they both felt more connected. She became Manager of the charity, leading her team to receive the prestigious Queen's Award for Voluntary Service in 2021, and winning an Outstanding Paper award in the Emerald Literati Awards in 2021 for a paper she co-authored about personalised care.

Chloe left work at the end of 2021 to home educate one of her sons after he was unable to settle in secondary school. She launched Hopscotch Coaching in October 2022, working with anyone who wants to take more time to look after their own health and wellbeing by tapping into their often lost fun, playful, creative sides - with a hop, skip and a jump!

Printed in Great Britain
by Amazon